# Rocket Ronnie
## AND THE VORTEX OF DOOM

Written by **Daniel Postgate**
Illustrated by **Pet Gotohda**

Published by Pearson Education Limited, Edinburgh Gate, Harlow, Essex, CM20 2JE
Registered company number: 872828

www.pearsonschools.co.uk

Text © Daniel Postgate 2011

Designed by Bigtop
Original illustrations © Pearson Education 2011
Illustrated by Pet Gotohda

The right of Daniel Postgate to be identified as author of this work has been asserted by him in accordance with the Copyright, Designs and Patents Act 1988.

First published 2011

15 14 13 12
10 9 8 7 6 5 4 3

**British Library Cataloguing in Publication Data**
A catalogue record for this book is available from the British Library

ISBN 978 0 435 91475 2

Printed and bound in Malaysia, CTP–PJB

**Acknowledgements**
We would like to thank the children and teachers of Bangor Central Integrated Primary School, NI; Bishop Henderson C of E Primary School, Somerset; Brookside Community Primary School, Somerset; Cheddington Combined School, Buckinghamshire; Cofton Primary School, Birmingham; Dair House Independent School, Buckinghamshire; Deal Parochial School, Kent; Newbold Riverside Primary School, Rugby and Windmill Primary School, Oxford for their invaluable help in the development and trialling of the Bug Club resources.

Every effort has been made to contact copyright holders of material reproduced in this book. Any omissions will be rectified in subsequent printings if notice is given to the publishers.

# Chapter 1
## The Guardians Make Contact

One afternoon, a girl named Veronica Witworth was making her way home from school. She was looking forward to playing her new computer game, *Asteroid Mayhem*, when something very strange happened. Something that would change her life forever.

Veronica had turned off the main street and was heading down an alley that led to the road where she lived. Suddenly a cloudy white light rose up in front of her like glowing smoke from an invisible bonfire. The light twisted and billowed around until it took the form of three shimmering figures in hooded robes. Veronica could hardly believe her eyes! She opened her mouth to speak but nothing came out. She was speechless.

One of the mysterious figures then spoke in a deep, slow voice. "We are the Guardians. We are an alien race from far across the galaxy – a race far more advanced than your own.

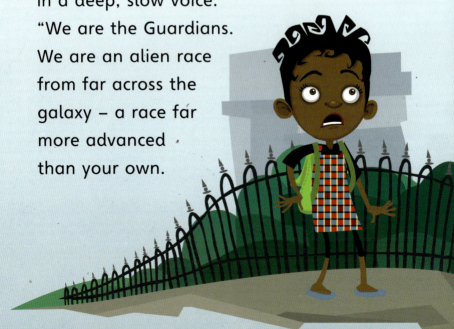

 The human race and this planet you call Earth are in danger from malicious alien forces. It is our job to help protect the human race so you can eventually join the Galactic Alliance and play an important part in bringing safety to everyone in the galaxy. That time has not yet come. Meanwhile, we need your help, Veronica Witworth."

Veronica managed to find her voice again. "W-w-what?" she stammered in disbelief.

"I said: We are the Guardians. We are an alien –"

"Yeah, OK, I get that bit," Veronica interrupted, "but why me? Why do you need *my* help?"

"We have been watching you and thousands of others like you. We needed to choose someone – just one human to help us in our task. We narrowed our choice down to just a few, and then, ultimately, we chose you," replied the figure, almost in a whisper, as if the dangerous forces might be listening in on their conversation.

"Oh, a bit like those talent shows on the telly?" suggested Veronica.

"Well, maybe, but I'm too busy to watch telly, especially Earth telly," muttered the figure. "Anyway, as I was saying, your computer game skills are excellent. You are thoughtful and imaginative. With your skills and our mind-bogglingly advanced technology, we can become a powerful force to protect your Planet Earth. So ... will you help us, Veronica Witworth?"

Veronica thought long and hard. She had never been asked to become the protector of the human race before, so she had to think carefully. What the Guardians were suggesting sounded dangerous, but it also sounded full of fun and adventure ... really, it wasn't a difficult decision to make.

"Okay, I'll do it!" she said finally.

"Good answer!" exclaimed the figure. "We will now prepare you for your task!"

Veronica felt something smooth in the palm of her hand and looked down to see that she was now holding a tiny, shiny phone which seemed to have appeared from nowhere.

"This is your contact console. You must keep it with you at all times so we are able to contact you whenever it is necessary. Now, please press the red button on the keypad."

Veronica did as she was asked. Her whole body started to tingle and fizz, and she felt strangely cold, as if she had been suddenly plunged into a vat of sparkling water.

Then she felt as if she
was shooting upwards at
tremendous speed. She tried
to cry out but her voice was
lost in the terrific roar which
engulfed her.

She shut her eyes tightly
and waited for it to be over.
Suddenly, all was silent and still.

Veronica opened one eye,
then the other. She was
standing in the centre of a
large, round room with an
oval window looking out onto
the stars and a small blue
and green planet swathed in
cloud. The room itself was shiny
and white with little lights set
into its walls that glowed and
twinkled with all the colours of
the rainbow.

"Galloping galaxies!" Veronica exclaimed, gazing around in bewilderment.

"Where am I?"

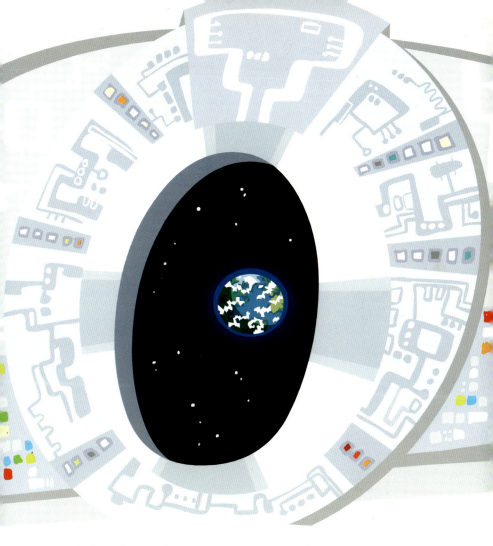

"You have been transported to our space station thousands of miles from Earth," echoed the voice of the Guardian. "This will be your headquarters. It is from here that you will go off on your missions into outer space."

"Outer space!" Veronica yelled. "How can I go off into … Jumping Jupiter!" Veronica had just noticed what she was wearing.

She slapped her hands on either side of the big plastic ball which engulfed her head.

"I've got a helmet on!" she shouted. "A space helmet!" Then she caught sight of her reflection in the oval window. She was in a red and grey space suit with grey gloves and boots, and it had a really chunky belt. She turned round to see some sort of power-pack on her back.

"Wow!" she whooped in excitement. "This is really cool!"

"You are no longer the schoolgirl Veronica Witworth," boomed the Guardian dramatically. "You are now Rocket Ronnie – Defender of the Human Race!"

"Oh yeah!" exclaimed Rocket Ronnie, punching the air with a gloved fist.

"Now it is time for me to leave," said the Guardian solemnly. "Goodbye, Rocket Ronnie. Defend your planet well. The people of Earth depend on you. And good luck!" The last words from the Guardian echoed around the room and then were gone.

"Hold on!" gasped Rocket Ronnie, suddenly feeling a bit frightened. "Come back! You can't just leave me here alone!"

*"You are not alone,"* said a voice ... a new voice. It was smooth, calm and female.

# Call me MAVIS.

"Who said that?" said Rocket Ronnie looking round the empty space station.

"*Me. I am your computerised Message And Vital Information Service – but you can call me MAVIS for short.*"

The new voice seemed to be coming from inside Rocket Ronnie's helmet.

"*I am an on-board computer, always ready to have a word in your ear when necessary.*"

"You sound like my mum," grinned Rocket Ronnie. "She's always having a word in my ear."

Rocket Ronnie was pleased and relieved to meet MAVIS – a talking computer was better company than no one at all. Then she heard a bleeping sound. She turned and nearly collided with something bobbing and hovering in the air. It was a smooth, silver globe, about the size of a bowling ball.

A little hole appeared in the ball and a metal stalk with a glowing orange ball on the end came out of it. It looked Rocket Ronnie up and down and then let out a low whistle.

"*This is your Special Investigation Device*," said MAVIS. "*You can call him SID. He will help you on your missions.*"

Rocket Ronnie shook her head and laughed. "A talking computer and a bleeping ball. The kids at school are never, *ever* going believe this!"

"*Nor should you tell them,*" said MAVIS gravely. "*What happens out here in space is absolutely top secret. No one from the human race must ever know. Not even your friends at school. Do you understand?*"

Rocket Ronnie nodded seriously.
"Message received and understood,"
she said.

Just at that moment, an alarm sounded
and the whole room glowed red.

*"Alert! Alert!"* said MAVIS, still in her
cool, calm voice. *"Our sensors indicate
a dangerous alien heading straight for
Planet Earth. Rocket Ronnie, it seems you
have arrived just in time."*

ALERT! ALERT!

## Chapter 3
### The Arrival of Vortex

"What shall I do now?" exclaimed Rocket Ronnie.

*"Use your skill and imagination, just as you do when you play one of your computer games,"* instructed MAVIS.

"But … but this isn't a computer game. It's real life!"

*"Ronnie, you were chosen for your skills,"* explained MAVIS calmly. *"We trust you. Now you need to trust yourself."*

"Yes, you're right," said Rocket Ronnie. "It's time for me to get tough."

*"I'm receiving a message from the alien, Ronnie,"* explained MAVIS. *"It's a satellite link. I'll put it on the screen right away."*

The oval window turned misty, then dark. Then the knobbly, purple face of a particularly ugly alien filled the screen.

He smirked unpleasantly at Rocket Ronnie. "Pitiful Earth Child," he said in a whining voice. "I am the Vortex of Doom! But you can call me Vortex. I am the most dangerous being in the galaxy. I have come to send you and all the people from Planet Earth into the void – a place of complete nothingness."

Then he threw back his head and howled with evil laughter.

"Erm, sorry to interrupt your laughing," broke in Rocket Ronnie, "but can I ask you a question?"

"Certainly," said Vortex. "Fire away!"

"Why?"

"Why what?" murmured Vortex.

"Why do you want to send people you don't know and have never met before to a place of nothingness?" Rocket Ronnie asked.

"Why?" whispered Vortex to himself, as if the question had never crossed his mind before.

"Oh yes, now I remember. It's because I am really nasty, and I really enjoy being nasty. I have absolutely no reason to be nasty. I just like it, that's all."

"Well, you're nothing but a big, pointless bully," said Rocket Ronnie angrily, "and you know what? Somebody needs to teach you a lesson, and that somebody is *me*!"

"Do your worst, little girl," Vortex sneered. Then the satellite link went dead.

*"Go, Rocket Ronnie! Go, Rocket Ronnie!"* chanted MAVIS, and SID bleeped in agreement.

A panel in the wall slid to one side, exposing an exit into the vast universe. Rocket Ronnie walked over to the edge of the station floor and stared out at the blackness. She hesitated for a moment, feeling slightly afraid.

Then she remembered she was now a super-hero and had to be brave.

"Come on, SID. Let's get out there," she stated boldly. She held her breath and stepped off into the unknown.

The moment her feet left the space station, the blasters in her jet-pack roared to life, sending her zooming out into star-speckled space. For a moment or two she found it hard to catch her breath. It was like the first time you jump into a swimming pool, or plunge into the sea. But within a few minutes she had got used to the strange sensation of weightlessness and had managed to learn how to control the blasters.

Rocket Ronnie was soon able to loop-the-loop and spin and twirl around as if she had been doing it all her life. "Hey, this is easy!" she yelled.

bleep!

bleep!

She heard a bleep and a squeak and
turned to see SID at her side. "Now, let's
go and sort out this Vortex chap!" she
cried and, with an extra blast, Rocket
Ronnie shot into the blackness.

As she approached Vortex, she saw that he was very large indeed. The nearer she got, the uglier Vortex appeared. Vortex was standing on a silver frisbee-like platform which seemed to be his transportation device. The strangest thing about him was the swirling hole at the centre of his large belly. It was dark – far darker than space. In fact, it was as black as black can be.

*"Watch out for that hole,"* MAVIS whispered in Rocket Ronnie's ear. *"That is his weapon. My sensors indicate that it is a type of black hole, with massive gravitational pull! It is very dangerous. If you are not careful, he will suck you into it!"*

"Thanks for the information," Rocket Ronnie replied. She felt a sudden tug and realised she was now too close to the gravitational pull of Vortex's ghastly hole.

She reacted immediately. In a split second she had navigated out of Vortex's range to a place of safety. "Hey Vortex!" she yelled, "We don't want you here. This is your last chance to leave peacefully. Will you go away and leave us alone?"

**"NEVER!"** Vortex yelled, and he let out a high-pitched cackle of laughter. "I'm not going anywhere, Earth Child!"

"I'm going to buzz around him, SID," Rocket Ronnie told her companion, "like a bee around a snapping dog. Hopefully, he'll lose his balance and fall off that frisbee thing."

Rocket Ronnie zoomed round and round Vortex, spinning and looping, while staying just out of reach of the alien's huge, flailing arms. She flew down around the huge alien's head, trying to annoy him so much that he would topple off his perch.

It was no good. Rocket Ronnie noticed that Vortex had straps on his boots that held him securely to his frisbee-like transportation device.

Suddenly Vortex managed to land a blow on Rocket Ronnie, sending her tumbling off into space.

"Now it's my turn!" squawked the laughing Vortex, blowing his chest out. As his cackling, howling laughter grew louder, the black hole on his belly started to grow larger and larger until it filled the whole of his torso and its gravitational pull grew stronger and stronger. Both Rocket Ronnie and SID found themselves being pulled by the incredible force. They began to tumble helplessly through space towards the enormous yawning abyss.

"This black hole is a portal to another universe," explained Vortex with delight. "A gateway to a universe where nothing exists – *absolutely nothing at all! Once you go though it, you can never return!*" His laugh became louder and even more unpleasant.

Rocket Ronnie was hurtling though space. She was being tossed about like a rag doll and was unable to think of anything she could do to save herself.

Any minute she would tumble into a nothingness from which she could never return. "Not a good way to start my career as a super-hero," she thought to herself.

Just as she was about to be pulled down into the hole itself, she managed to grab onto Vortex's arm. She held on to it with all her might.

"Hey, get off my arm, you little pest!" yelled Vortex, but no matter how hard the alien shook, Rocket Ronnie managed to hold on.

SID came flying past and, just before he vanished into the void, he managed to shoot out a telescopic metal arm and clutch onto his companion. Then he hauled himself up and Ronnie held him tightly under her arm like a rugby ball.

"We'll get out of this somehow," she assured her new friend, "although right now I don't know how."

The force of the pull on Rocket Ronnie was colossal – like a hurricane but a hundred times stronger. She felt her grip on Vortex's arm start to weaken. Time was running out for her and her metallic friend.

"I must think of a way out. There must be a way," Rocket Ronnie muttered to herself through gritted teeth.

"If the black hole pulls in everything, then it must be able to pull ... that's it! Even Vortex can't escape the black hole!"

She spoke to the on-board computer in a loud and clear voice. "MAVIS! Set my blasters to full power, now!"

*"All right, Ronnie,"* said MAVIS in her usual calm voice, although she did sound a little bit flustered. *"There's no need to shout."*

The blasters howled to full power. Even through the thick material of her space suit, Rocket Ronnie could feel their scalding heat against the backs of her legs. The force of the blasters exactly matched the force of Vortex's black hole. They were caught, with neither power able to overwhelm the other. However, Rocket Ronnie's blasters could not go on forever. The fuel would eventually run out.

Fortunately, Rocket Ronnie had a plan. She just needed that little bit more thrust to pull them free. Gripping Vortex's arm as tightly as she could, she gave it one almighty push. The force was just enough to push SID and her free. They shot upwards like a couple of missiles, back into the safety of their own galaxy.

Rocket Ronnie turned to see what had become of Vortex. By pushing on Vortex's arm the girl had swung his arm forward into the black hole. The alien was caught by the pull of his own weapon.

"Aaaaargh!" cried Vortex as he desperately tried to pull his arm free.

He stared wide-eyed at Rocket Ronnie as beads of sweat drizzled down his face. "Beaten by a snivelling little kid!" he screeched. "How embarrassing! You may have won this time, Earth Child, but I'll be back. I'm going nowhere!" Then Vortex gave up the fight with the black hole.

He spun round and round, ever faster, as though he was in an enormous washing machine on spin-cycle.

Then, quite extraordinarily, he disappeared altogether. There was nothing left of him at all. He had completely vanished into his own black hole, and the black hole – as it was part of him – had vanished too.

"Cart-wheeling comets! That was close!" exclaimed Rocket Ronnie with a sigh of relief. "I hope that's the last we'll see of him!"

Pfffffff!

SID let out a triumphant hoot and his whole orb glowed bright white with the satisfaction of a job well done.

"Come on, SID. Let's get back to the space station," said Ronnie.

Rocket Ronnie brought her blasters down to a gentle hiss as she lightly stepped back onto the floor of the space station and the panel behind her slid closed. She was glad to feel something solid beneath her feet again. SID was glad to be back too. He let out a grateful buzz and rolled onto the floor, clearly exhausted.

"*Well, Rocket Ronnie. I think you did very well – very well indeed. Congratulations!*" said MAVIS. "*The Guardians certainly chose wisely when they chose you.*"

"Yes, I suppose I did do rather well," grinned Rocket Ronnie with her hands on her hips.

"*Hmm, well don't get too pleased with yourself,*" MAVIS warned. "*There will soon be other aliens, and they might not be quite as easy to deal with as that big purple fool.*"

"Easy?" spluttered Rocket Ronnie. "By the moons of Mars, you're a hard computer to please."

MAVIS let out a short, crisp laugh. "*Goodbye for now, Rocket Ronnie,*" she said, smoothly. "*It's time for you to become plain Veronica Witworth again.*"

Goodbye for now, Rocket Ronnie.

Rocket Ronnie felt the tingling and fizzing in her body again. She closed her eyes tightly and let the coldness sweep through her and the roar fill her ears.

A moment later, she was standing in the alley where she had first met the mysterious hooded figure. The space suit had gone and she was back in her usual school clothes. For a moment, she wondered if it had all been some kind of crazy dream. Then she checked her pocket. Her fingers felt the tiny, shiny phone. She took it out and looked at it. Written on its screen, she read:

UNTIL THE NEXT TIME.

Veronica ran down the alley, into the road where she lived, and soon arrived at her house. She pushed open the door, just in time to see her mum putting her tea on the table. It was her favourite – fish fingers, baked beans and salad.

"You're a bit late," said her mum. "What kept you?"

"Nothing, Mum," said Veronica with a secret smile. *"Absolutely nothing at all."*